The A to Z Book of Wildflowers

By
Michael P. Earney

Cover Illustration: The use of Queen Anne's Lace for the cover illustration may offend purists who would rather see a true native Texas wildflower. However, Queen Anne's Lace, like so many invasive species, has become part of the landscape. Tumbleweed, or Russian thistle, came from Russia but what could be more archetypically American than this plant which rolls through so many Western movies and piles up against the fences cattlemen erected throughout the west?

Special thanks to Susan Sander with the Riverside Nature Center in Kerrville, Texas, Joe Marcus at the Ladybird Johnson Flower Center in Austin, Texas, and Carol Elliott, for their invaluable input and knowledgeable insights.

ISBN-13: 978-1-941345-64-1 HB
ISBN-13: 978-1-941345-65-8 PB

ERIN GO BRAGH
Publishing
Canyon Lake, TX
www.ErinGoBraghPublishing.com

Plants

If plants could talk, they'd never stop, they have so much to tell!
They know the story of the earth and sky,
They know the birds, they know the bees,
They know the butterfly!

There are plants that walk, plants that climb,
Plants that live beneath the waves,
Plants that float across the seas,
And even plants that fly!

Plants heal the sick
And give us all our daily bread.
They house us, clothe us, keep us warm
And cook the food that they provide.

Since first we came into this world
They've given us the air we breathe.
In simple truth without the plants
Mankind could not survive!

Their beauty is beyond compare—
A multitude of colors, shapes and sizes
With fragrant scents that fill the air.
In humble gratitude for all they share
Let us as one our voices raise
For evermore to sing their praise.

Michael P. Earney
2016

Rachel Carson's *Silent Spring,* published in 1962, brought environmental concerns into public view. The use of pesticides was shown to have deadly effects not only on wildlife but on humans too. Today the use of pesticides and herbicides continues to have devastating effects on our environment. The Environmental Protection Agency lacks the power or will to control the chemicals that penetrate our entire ecosystem. While it is evident pest controls are necessary in order to sustain agriculture on the levels needed to feed the world's population, the mutation and disappearance of wild plants, animals, birds, and insects is of concern to everyone. It is an issue that must be addressed before it is too late!

I hope you enjoy this book.
You can let me know at: facebook.com/michaelpearney37
or linkedin.com/pub/michael-earney
or visit my website: **www.MichaelEarney.com**
Tell your friends and please review my book on Amazon, Goodreads, or any other review site. Thank you!

The A to Z Book of Wildflowers

There are so many wildflowers to see! From tiny, tiny belly-flowers (the ones you have to lie on your stomach to see,) to the large and showy. It can be hard to keep their names straight at times, so this book is an attempt to help with at least a few of them. We are not going to go into families, genera or species too much, though you will see the common name and the scientific or Latin name of each. Since I am living in Texas where there are over 5,000 species of flowering plants, many will be common to this state but most have a large range so you will just as likely see them elsewhere. Some are quite rare, or flower for a very short period of time at certain times of the year and only if the conditions are right. These are the difficult ones, but that is part of the joy of wildflowers—the chance to see them in flower is such a gift. I once made a journey from Santa Fe, New Mexico to Big Bend National Park in Texas to see flowers, some of which had not bloomed in 25 years, some others not in 50 years. Usually, we are lucky in that if we miss them this year they will be back next year. I predict that once you start noticing the wildflowers you will see more and more. Those tiny insignificant ones right under your feet, the ones that blossom unseen in hard to reach places and that one, when you do see it, you can't believe you never noticed it before. It is because so much in nature goes unnoticed and unappreciated that we set about changing the landscape, bring in alien species, divert resources and generally alter our surroundings. We need to remind ourselves of the great beauty around us that nobody planted, no one waters or weeds, and no one can say, "Those are mine." They belong to us all.

n.b. I have generally left out sizes and physical descriptions of the plants since the text is accompanied by the illustration. Of course there are lookalikes, but part of the fun of discovery is in learning to distinguish one from another without being told. You don't have to become a botanist to appreciate wildflowers; just stop more often and take a longer look. That's what I did.

Michael P. Earney Utopia, Texas 2018

A is for

ANEMONE
Wind Flower

Michael Emry

A is for ANEMONE, Wind Flower, Crowfoot family (Ranunculaceae)

Anemones are among the earliest flowers to bloom in the spring. Almost lost in the dead grasses of winter they slowly push their way into the light, opening as the day begins, then closing at night or if it becomes cloudy. With its leaves at the base except for two or three leaflets near the top of the stalk; the ten-petal anemone is about one inch across, mostly white, on the end of a long stalk; sometimes with touches of pink, blue or purple, usually on the underside. It seldom has less than 12 or 14 petals which are not really petals but sepals. At times these will have enough color to be mistaken for the Carolina anemone which has more sepals, is wider across and has more color but a far shorter fruiting head, the feature which allows you to distinguish between them. Why is it called the ten-petal anemone? Well, those sepals sure look like petals, and it was probably named before botanists drew the distinction. The state flower of South Dakota is an anemone, *Anemone patens* or pasque-flower. The name refers to the Paschal, or Easter, time of year when the anemone blooms.

Cool Fact: *Anemone* derives from *anemonos,* Greek for "daughter of the wind." When there was less known about how nature works, the impression the flowers opened with the spring breezes made people think the wind opened the flowers.

What other wildflowers start with A?

B is for

BLUEBELL
Gentian family

B is for BLUEBELL, Gentian family, *Eustoma exaltatum* spp. *Russellianum*, also called purple prairie gentian and lira de San Pedro.
Pronunciation; yoo-STOH-mah ex-al-TAT-um

Bluebells grow in moist, sunny places. I first saw them growing in Blanco County in the Texas Hill Country; beside a creek below the man-made dam of a cattle watering hole (called a 'tank' in Texas). For the next twenty years I never saw them there again. They are some of the most beautiful wildflowers and I hope you will get to see them. The flowers, on branched, slender stems, can be four inches high and up to two inches across. The plants can stand over two feet high. Now the Texas Bluebell, *Campanula reverchonii* is very rare—found exclusively in Mason, Burnet and Llano counties—and really should be protected. Look for the Venus Looking Glass in this genus too. Unlike the Texas bluebell, bluebells belonging to different families generally hang down and look like bells. The Mountain bluebell is edible; the flowers and leaves can be eaten raw or cooked. The Cheyenne Indians used it in an infusion for smallpox and measles. In England, which is home to more than half the world's bluebells, (although theirs are in a different genus, *Hyacinthoides),* bluebells carpet the woodlands when they flower. People throw themselves down in them and pick huge bunches. This practice has caused this Bluebell to be named a protected species in England and Scotland.

Cool Fact: Long before the English bluebell became a protected species they were sometimes known as Dead Man's Bells because fairies were thought to cast spells on those who dared to pick or damage them. Where are the fairies now that we need them?

What other wildflowers start with B?

C is for CHOLLA

Cylindropuntia imbricata

C is for CHOLLA, (Cactaceae) aka Tree cholla, Cane cholla, Walking stick cholla, *Cylindropuntia imbricata* var. *arborescens*
Pronunciation; oh-PUN-shah im-breh-KAH-tah

Cholla cactus you expect to see in Arizona and New Mexico but the western third of Texas has its fair share. It looks more like a shrub than a tree but it can get up to 12 feet high, making it the tallest cactus in Texas. It usually flowers May through June. The flowers open before mid-day and, as with a lot of cacti, last only one day. Native American tribes of the Southwest ate the flower buds and fruits. The seeds can be roasted and ground for food. The young stems, if you want to go to the trouble of removing the tiny spines, are edible too. It's not hard to identify though there is a look-alike species, *O. imbricata* var. *argentea*, that doesn't grow as big and is confined to a tiny part of the Big Bend National Park. The Christmas cholla community, also known as pencil cactus, is seen more often as it grows over a large part of Texas and is cultivated as an ornamental in gardens. Some of the low, creeping cholla can be hard to identify as cholla but there are a number of them and are well worth the effort to find.

Cactus fanciers have annihilated some cacti in their native habitats. Many collectors are ruthless in their pursuit. Once while in Big Bend I saw people illegally gathering cactus and called the Park service who immediately sent someone to apprehend the thieves.

Cool Fact: Long stems of the Tree cholla, dried and with the fleshy outer coating removed along with the spines, are used as walking sticks and for making ornamental furniture and fences. In Mexico cuttings are planted in a row to grow into a living fence that will keep out just about everything except the birds nesting in them.

What other wildflowers start with C?

D is for

DEATH CAMAS

Zigadenis nuttallii

Michael Eanny

D is for DEATH CAMAS, *Zigadenis nuttallii,* (Liliaceae), White-lily

Death Camas. The name should be warning enough but because it looks so much like the edible and rather tasty wild onion, which is in the same family, it can't be stressed too often to watch out. That name is not there for nothing; the Death camas is deadly poisonous. The thing to remember when you are looking for wild onions to eat is, if they don't smell like onions they aren't onions and you must not eat them. So, get to know this member of the lily family along with others, like the day lily, tiger lily, green lily and many more because they are most striking to see. Though again, some plants called lilies are not in the lily family. Aloe vera is a member and like others in the family has been used for thousands of years for healing. Its skin softening ability has given it a place in lotions, salves, creams and shampoos. It also shows up a lot in crossword puzzles. So, try to identify the Death Camas and remember that, as in all families, there is the good and the bad.

n.b. Delena Tull puts the death camas in the *Melanthiaceae*-False-Hellebore family

Cool Fact: Chicago comes from the Indian word *Shikata,* which meant "place where the wild onions are strong smelling."

What other wildflowers start with D?

E is for

EVENING PRIMROSE
Oenothera elata

E

is for EVENING PRIMROSE, *Oenothera elata* spp. *Hirsutissima,* (Oneagraceae), Giant evening primrose

Evening Primroses are in a different family from Primroses. They are neither primroses nor roses, though they smell as sweet. The evening primroses found in Texas come in yellow, white, pink, beach and desert -- wait, are those last two colors? There's also the Stemless, Cut-Leaf, Water and Four-Point. I could go on but then we get into family, species, variety, etc. and head off in all kinds of directions. I will mention the Square-Bud Primrose since you have probably seen it. It's the bright yellow one that has the black throat and black stigma. None of the other evening primroses have flowers quite as large as the giant, hence the name. They do mostly open in the evening and stay open all night, so that long-tongued moths like the Hawk moth can visit and get pollen on themselves as they go for the nectar. Then they spread that stuff around to the other flowers ensuring we will get to see more evening primroses next year. Now, wouldn't you know it, the Pink evening primrose stays open during the day. Just like the names, it's sometimes hard to keep the habits of the evening primroses straight.

Cool Fact: The flowers, roots and tender new leaves can be eaten and have long been used by Native Americans for medicine. They may prove useful for treating arthritis.

What other wildflowers start with E?

F is for

FOXGLOVE
Penstemon cobaea

F

F is for FOXGLOVE, *Penstemon cobaea*, Figwort family,
Witch's Glove, Fairies glove, Fairy caps, Foxbell, Lion's mouth

Foxglove, wild foxglove or false foxglove (*Penstemon cobaea, to* be perfectly clear about this), is a beautiful flower. When seen growing in a ditch or by the side of the highway it makes one think it must have escaped from a garden because it looks like a cultivated plant. Of course, the cultivated varieties are even more showy with their tall cascades of bell shaped flowers, but they are in a different family. Not that the figwort family, *Scrophulariaceae,* doesn't have a lot of beautiful members. It's hard to keep up with them sometimes. The scarlet, red and Havard penstemon tend to stand out even though their flowers are fairly small. Wild foxglove, being the largest flowered penstemon, most resembles the garden variety to my mind. Its upturned open mouth with the lined lower lip just invites insects in for a nectar 'pick-me-up' adding, "Oh, and on the way out, please take some pollen next door, would you?" Some foxgloves have dots leading inside but the message is the same, "come on in!" Then there is the 3 to 6 feet high Cenizo, or purple sage, (cenizo means ashy and the leaves are gray-green). That a bush this size could be related to foxglove seems unlikely, but those botanists are on top of it. Native Americans found ways to use this family as medicine but it was an English doctor who in 1785 worked out ways to extract digitalis from the foxglove plant, (a *Digitalis* spp), for the prevention of heart failure.

Cool Fact: In English folk-lore there is an explanation for the name foxglove. It says bad fairies originally gave the soft flowers to foxes to wear so that when they sneaked into chicken coops, their steps would be muffled and the rooster wouldn't wake up to warn the hens.

What other wildflowers start with F?

G

is for
Gaillardia pulchella
Indian Blanket

Michael Earny

G

is for *Gaillardia pulchella,* Composite family, Indian Blanket, Blanket Flower, Firewheel, Sunburst, Bandana Daisy
Pronunciation; gur-LAR-dee-yah pul-CHELL-ah

Gaillardia pulchella is the Latin or genus name for Indian Blanket. Its appearance following the spring flowers is a sign that summer is now on its way. There are a number of *Gaillardia* in Texas, though *G. pulchella* is the most common. It and the Red Gaillardia are the only two that are annuals, the rest are perennial. It does literally blanket the fields after the bluebonnets have faded away. I'm sure you can understand why it is called Firewheel. The bright red center of the flowers and the glowing yellow tips really stand out. All Gaillardia are native to America and can be found from Missouri and Nebraska to Louisiana and Texas. It's a member of the Sunflower family. Can you imagine what it would be like if pre-Columbian Indians had domesticated this family member instead of the sunflower? What huge Firewheels we would have!

Cool Fact: Legend has it the flower was originally pure yellow and much favored by the Aztec. When the invading Spanish conquistadors attacked and slaughtered the Mexican natives, the story tells as victims fell the blood of those people, who loved the flower so much, was caught up in its cup where it remains to this day.

What other wildflowers start with G?

H is for HONEYSUCKLE
Lonicera

Michael Emry

H is for HONEYSUCKLE, *Lonicera* spp, Honeysuckle Family, Caprifoliaceae

Honeysuckle gets its name from the fact you can pick one and suck the little drop of honey sweet liquid in the center. Naturally bees, butterflies, and hummingbirds find it tasty too. As they go after that drop of sweetness they pick up pollen and carry it on to the next flower, thus ensuring the plant will fruit. Some honeysuckle berries are highly toxic, others are considered edible, but best just to stick to that honey drop.

While there is a bush honeysuckle, most honeysuckles are vines that depend upon other plants or inanimate objects for support. The coral honeysuckle, also known as the trumpet honeysuckle, is native to Texas but ranges east to Florida and north into Nebraska, Massachusetts and Connecticut. The leaves grow in pairs with the pair under the flowers and often the next pair down, melding together to form a disc-like shape. The invasive Japanese honeysuckle will clamber over entire groves of trees, destroying them. Such invaders were meant for the garden but have strayed into the wild where they compete with the native plants. So, look for the wild honeysuckle and help it where you can. It can be transplanted; best in early spring before it buds out or in the fall when it is going dormant; or take cuttings and propagate those. You can also plant honeysuckle seeds, just make sure they're from the wild honeysuckle and not one of those invaders.

Cool Fact: Phillip Freneau (1752-1832) was a friend of James Madison and Thomas Jefferson. Jefferson hired him as editor of the National Gazette, a partisan paper that upset a lot of politicians, including President George Washington. He also wrote poetry. His poem "The Wild Honeysuckle" is an early example of the nature poem:

Fair flower, that dost so comely grow, Hid in this silent, dull retreat,
Untouched thy honied blossoms blow, Unseen thy little branches greet:
No roving foot shall crush thee here, No busy hand provoke a tear.

What other wildflowers start with H?

I is for

IPOMOEA
Morning Glory

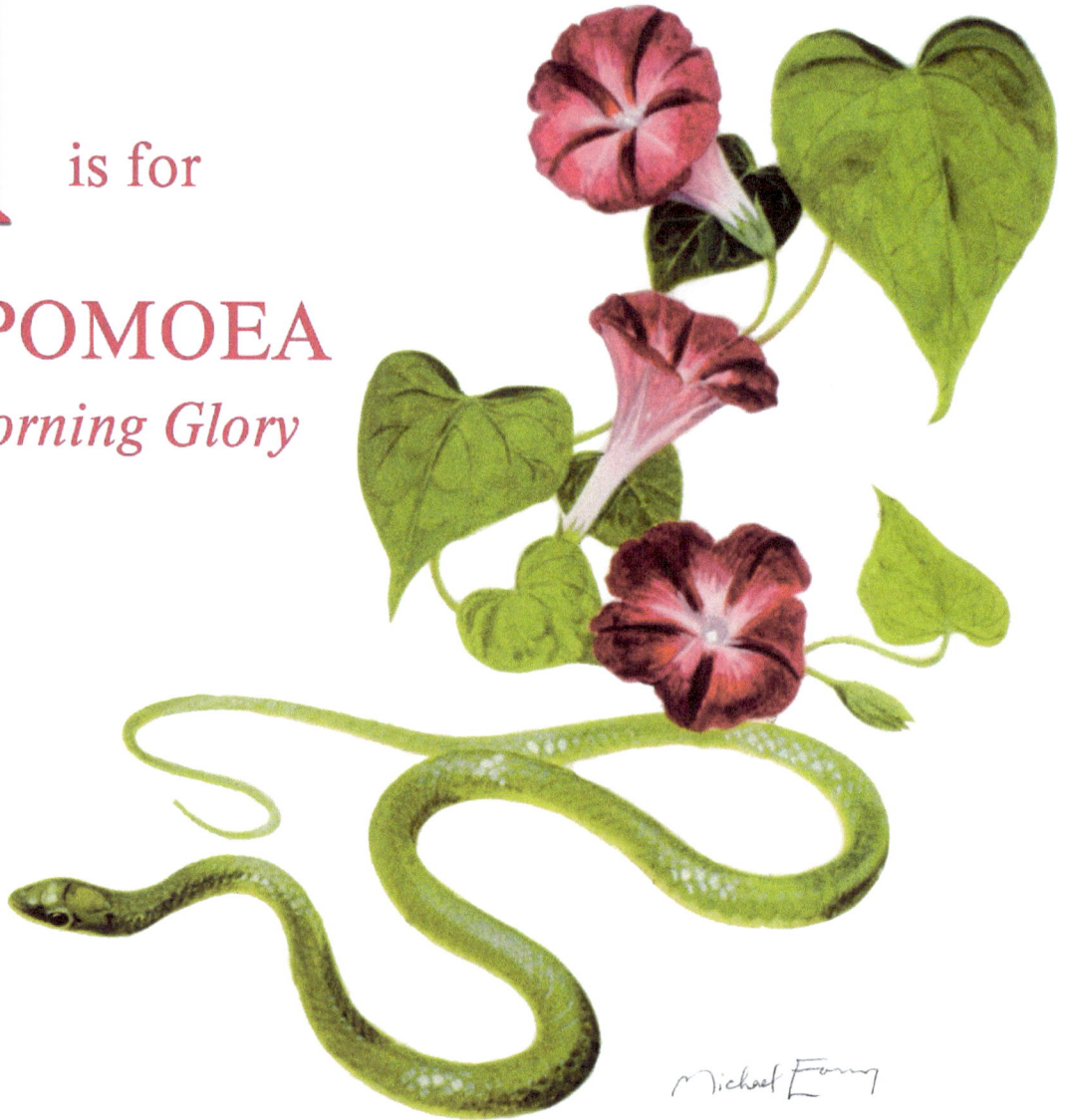

I is for *IPOMOEA,* (Convolvulaceae), Morning glory, Bindweed, Tie Vine, Dodder, Love Vine

Ipomoea is where we find the morning glory, a mostly twining, creeping, sprawling or climbing plant. It will twine its tendrils around anything it can. You will see them covering a mailbox or taking over a fence. It will keep growing up as long as there is support; trees, telephone poles, it doesn't care, so long as it's up. The morning glory's profusion of bright funnel-shaped flowers, from white, yellow, pale blue, and onto scarlet and purple, make it attractive for cultivation. However, its tendency to take over has earned it some unpleasant names: strangle weed, witch's shoelaces, and devil's garters being just a few. Bindweed, which is shown here, makes a pretty display but it's one of those that can be a nuisance. The rare Shrub morning glory is found only in the Big Bend National Park in Texas where invasive non-native species plague its habitat.

Salt-marsh morning glory, Beach morning glory (known as Goat-foot or Goat's foot morning glory) all do a fine job helping to stabilize the coastal dunes. The wild potato is also in this family and was once used extensively by Native Americans for food. It has many medicinal properties, being used throughout the world for a variety of ailments, from urinary tract infections to lung problems. The seeds of one tropical morning glory are used in religious ceremonies of indigenous people in Latin America to produce the hallucinations that are an integral part of their curing rituals, it also allows the user to foretell the future.

Cool Fact: The Morning glory twines in a counter-clockwise direction while many other vines twine clockwise. When the morning glory and one of these other vines meet they twine tightly around each other, one of the reasons why the Morning glory is called the love vine.

What other wildflowers start with I?

P.S. That Smooth Green Snake in the picture is not poisonous. It won't harm you so please don't harm it if you come upon one.

J is for

JIMSON
WEED
Datura

J is for JIMSONWEED, *Datura* spp. Nightshade Family, (Solanaceae), Thorn Apple

Pronunciation; day-TOO-rah

Jimsonweed, a corruption of Jamestown weed, has become attached to more than just the *Datura stramonium* that was eaten by Royalist soldiers during the 1676 colonial uprising in Jamestown, Virginia. Those men had cooked up the greens, but all parts of the plant are toxic. The soldiers were hallucinating and acting crazy for several days! Just a few grams can kill a child. The *Solanum* genus includes tomatoes, potatoes, bell peppers, and let's not forget, tobacco. It took many years for Europeans to accept that you could eat such members of the nightshade family as tomatoes and potatoes that came from the Americas but they finally caught on even though they are toxic. You should never eat the green part of potatoes, peel it off if you see some. Tobacco, if you didn't know, has one of the most highly toxic alkaloids known—nicotine. Those large 6" to 9" long horn-shaped flowers, erect on the common Datura, bloom at night and are pollinated by the Hawk moth and the Hummingbird moth. The shrubs or small trees with long hanging, colorful flowers belong to a distinct genus, *Brugmansia*. *Datura wrightii* is native to America, it's known as the sacred Datura and as the thorn apple for its large round prickly seed pods. As with the rest of the family, all parts are poisonous though it is used by some indigenous groups in rituals under very strictly controlled conditions.

Cool Fact: Some countries prohibit the buying, selling or cultivation of *Datura*. It is considered to be a noxious weed having no economic purpose and being harmful to humans and animals. In spite of this (because of its impressive display of flowers), the *Brugmansia* is found in gardens throughout the world.

What other wildflowers start with J?

K is for

KENTUCKY
LADY'S SLIPPER
Cypripedium kentuckiense

Michael Emery

K is for KENTUCKY LADY'S SLIPPER, *Cypripedium kentuckiense,* Orchid Family, Southern Lady's Slipper

Kentucky Lady's Slipper is a rare plant in Texas. The other southern states where it is found—Alabama, Arkansas, Georgia, Kentucky, Louisiana, Mississippi, Oklahoma, Tennessee and Virginia—also have only small, isolated populations confined to very particular habitats, primarily hardwood forests near water. It is a perennial and flowers late March through May. There are many other Lady's Slippers to which it's related. The Showy Lady's Slipper is the State flower of Minnesota. Lady's Slippers are in the orchid family, one of the world's largest and most interesting plant families. There are over 10,000 species of orchid but only 140 grow in North America. The fruit of the Lady's Slipper has abundant but tiny seeds from which it's exceedingly difficult to grow new plants. They do not transplant well and grow slowly. If you should be lucky enough to find them, please leave this lovely, interesting plant alone.

Cool Fact: The Aztecs called it, tlilxochitl (t-lil-SHOCK-itle.) The Spanish called it vainilla, "little pod". "Vaina" means "pod". "Illa" denotes smallness (except in the case of Godzilla). From this we have "vanilla". The word vanilla is often used to denote ordinary or boring, but the vanilla bean is the second most expensive spice available after saffron! When you have vanilla ice cream you are eating a little bit of a very expensive orchid. (If it isn't in fact a synthetic flavoring.)
n.b. Vanilla is native to the Americas. It is pollinated by a quite rare stingless bee. Commercial vanilla is mostly now grown in Madagascar and Indonesia. The bee wasn't transplanted so in those countries each vanilla flower has to be individually hand pollinated to produce a single bean. Most vanilla extract is alcohol that has been infused with vanilla beans.

What other wildflowers start with K?

L is for LEGUMINOSAE

Bluebonnet

Michael Emery

L

is for LEGUME, (Leguminosae), Bluebonnet, *Lupinus texensis*
Pronunciation: loo-PYE-nus tex-EN-sis

Legumes form one of the largest family of plants in the world and are one of the most economically important. All the beans and peas we eat as well as peanuts come from these plants. Lupines are in this family which is why the bluebonnet, the State flower of Texas, is shown here. If you look closely you will see the bluebonnet exhibits the telltale characteristics of most legumes—the pea flower shape. It has bilateral symmetry; one side is the mirror image of the other. The Redbud has heart shaped leaves, but the flower has the common pea flower shape and its pods are edible. Even the acacias and mesquites with the puffball type of flower, have the characteristic pea or bean pod, so it's not hard to distinguish them. However, don't think they're all edible! Texas mountain laurel or mescal bean and locoweed are both part of this family. They have different leaves but the same flower shape. Both are deadly poisonous. The red beans of the mountain laurel should not be eaten. And locoweed? You don't want to see what that will do to a horse. Native Americans once used the poisonous varieties for catching fish and for medicine. The Mescalero Apache were known for using the mescal bean in religious ceremonies. Its toxicity produces hallucinations.

Cool Fact: Lady Bird Johnson inspired more than 200 environmental laws signed during her husband's administration. She was responsible for the use of native plants along America's highways. Ironically, people now drive their polluting automobiles around just to see the profusions of bluebonnets and other wildflowers that appear in the spring. It was her vision which brought about the Lady Bird Johnson Wildflower Center in Austin, Texas. There the sustainable use and conservation of wildflowers, plants, and landscapes—that minimize the need for fertilizers and herbicides—is practiced and taught. They have more than 700 native species on display.

What other wildflowers start with L?

M is for

MILKWEED

Asclepias

Michael Emery

M is for MILKWEED, *Asclepias* species Milkweed Family, (Asclepiadaceae)

Milkweeds are poisonous. Some species are toxic enough to kill sheep or goats. Livestock and even turkeys will sicken if they should eat it. Green milkweed, *A. asperula*, shown here is among the most highly toxic species. Usually poisonings occur when overgrazing has removed better forage. Chemical companies are developing stronger and stronger herbicides to eradicate the milkweed. This may please some ranchers but is a very bad thing because, though some animals do die each year, the milkweed is essential to the life cycle of the Monarch butterfly. On its way from Mexico, heading north, the monarch lays its eggs on the leaves of the milkweed, the caterpillars that emerge from these eggs feed on the plant and absorb the plant's toxins. These are passed on to the adult butterfly. In one of those mysteries of nature, birds know not to eat the monarch. Stranger yet, the Viceroy butterfly mimics the monarch in its color pattern so as to avoid becoming dinner for any bird! Already threatened by the loss of its winter home in Mexico due to illegal logging, the eradication of milkweed in this country would mean the loss of one of the most beautiful butterflies we have. You may not find the flowers of the milkweed particularly attractive but the monarch butterfly loves them!

Cool Fact: *Asclepias* comes from the Greek god of medicine, Asklepios. That's because milkweed has been used as a medicine for hundreds of years to treat a wide variety of ailments from cuts to rheumatism. Remember the old saying, "What doesn't kill you will make you strong!"

What other wildflowers start with M?

N is for

NIGHTSHADE
Solanaceae

$\mathcal{N}$ is for NIGHTSHADE, *Solanum elaeagnifolium,* Silver-leaf Nightshade, Tomato weed, Nightshade Family, (Solanaceae)

Nightshade takes us back to the Solanaceae. Remember Jimson Weed, potatoes, tomatoes, tobacco? Silver-leaf nightshade is one of the more poisonous members of the family. The leaves and fruit can poison animals if they ingest only 0.1- 0.3 percent of their body weight of this plant, though some birds and small mammals eat the berries with no ill effect. Once the Spanish had imported cows, sheep and goats, the Pima Indians of Arizona found they could make cheese from their milk, using crushed ripe berries of the silver-leaf as a vegetarian rennet. Thistle, nettle, and mallow can be used in the same way. Regular rennet, used to curdle milk, comes from the fourth stomach of young ruminants, such as calves and lambs. The cheese is called Asadero, Oaxaca or Chihuahua queso, and Quesillo. The silver-leaf nightshade will colonize overgrazed, disturbed or unmanaged areas as the creeping roots can grow very deep and produce shoots six feet away from the parent plant. Add to this the seeds it drops and you soon have a monster. It is native throughout most of Texas and banned as a noxious weed in some States. The tiny hairs on the leaves and stems give the silvery-green effect. Those on the stem turn to prickles when the plant matures. The ripe yellow berries look pretty appealing but best leave them alone, unless you plan to make some cheese.

Cool Fact: The name Pima is believed to come from *pi'añi mac, pi-mac,* or *pinimahch,* meaning, "No" or "I don't know," a phrase used repeatedly by the Othama (as the Pima called themselves) in their initial meetings with Europeans. A lot of Indian tribe names came about due to similar misunderstandings, beginning with Columbus thinking he was in India.

What other wildflowers start with N?

O

is for **OPUNTIA**

Prickly Pear Cactus

O is for OPUNTIA. Prickly Pear Cactus, Nopal, *Opuntia engelmanii* var. *lindheimeri,* Cactus Family (Cactaceae)

Opuntia is arguably the most common cactus. It is definitely the most widespread. There are 114 species in Mexico alone and more than 50 in the United States. The *Opuntia engelmannii* var. *lindheimeri* is certainly the most widespread in Texas. It is the State plant of Texas. Also known as nopal and tuna, it loves to take over areas that have been overgrazed, i.e. much of Texas, unfortunately. Being more drought resistant than most other plants it thrives where others have given up. It's not the prettiest of prickly pears but when it flowers, usually March through June, it looks spectacular. Nopal comes from the Nahuatl word "nohpali," the Aztec name for the pads and the whole plant. Nopalitos, (ito and illa are both diminutives added to indicate smallness) are the tender young pads that grow each year on the old nopals. Gathered and cleaned of their tiny spines, nopalitos are sliced up and served with all kinds of Mexican dishes. The tuna is the "pear" that grows along the edge (as well as on the face) of the nopales. They can be eaten green or after they turn red. Nopal is known to lower blood pressure and is used for treating type-2 diabetes. For more about Opuntia see, *The A to Z book of Weeds and Other Useful Plants.*

Cool Fact: At one time, in parts of Latin America, a mash of boiled Opuntia would be used to filter water but the practice fell out of use. Now the University of Florida in Tampa is working on producing a water filter using the same material, cactus goop.

What other wildflowers start with O?

P

is for

PAINTBRUSH

Castilleja indivisa

Michael Emery

P

P is for PAINTBRUSH, *Castilleja indivisa,* Texas paintbrush, Indian Paintbrush, Figwort Family (Scrophulariaceae)
Pronunciation kass-the-LAY-ah in-duh-VEE-zah

Paintbrush grows alongside the Bluebonnet in the spring. Thousands of pounds of both plants' seeds are sown along the Texas highways. Since there are over five million seeds to a pound it's not hard to understand why so many can be seen along our highways in the spring. Of course, its name comes from the idea that the sepals and red tipped leafy bracts, which contain the flowers, resemble a brush dipped in red paint. It's interesting that a plant whose flower is almost completely hidden should prove to be one of the most popular wildflowers in Texas. Several different colored Paintbrush can be found across the western states. The Western Paintbrush has a mix of red and yellow. The Yellow Paintbrush and the Purple Paintbrush are grouped under the name, Prairie Paintbrush *Castilleja purpurea,* together with an orange variation. These all grow in the Texas Hill Country where you won't find much prairie. In Wyoming, *Castilleja linariaefolia*, Indian Paintbrush, is the State flower. The Texas, or Scarlet Paintbrush, is an annual, hence the need for all those seeds. Texas has eight other species of *Castilleja* that are perennials. A greenish yellow dye is obtained from the stems, leaves and flowers. Native Americans used it to dye cotton and wool for weaving. It was also made into a weak tea to treat rheumatism and provided remedies for other ailments.

Cool Fact: It seems the Paintbrush is hemiparasitic. In times of need it apparently taps into the roots of nearby plants to draw water and minerals. Though they look great together, the Bluebonnet may not love its neighbor quite as much as we do.

What other wildflowers start with P?

Q is for QUEEN ANNE'S LACE

Daucus carota

Q is for QUEEN ANNE'S LACE, *Daucus carota,* Birds Nest, Bishop's Lace, Wild Carrot, Carrot Family (Apiaceae)

Queen Anne's lace is the non-native wild carrot that's been around for thousands of years, being used medicinally all that time. The carrots we know today were more than likely bred from it. Because of its strong resemblance to other family members like poison hemlock, the poisonous water hemlock, and fools' parsley— my friend Delena Tull discourages using any of the wild carrots, while Euell Gibbons, always the adventurous one, enjoyed eating it and heartily recommended it. However, you must be careful and the best test is to crush the leaves of whatever plant you have come upon and sniff. The wild carrot will smell like carrot and the hemlocks will smell nasty. There are other characteristics to check if you are still not sure. Look for the dark red flower in the center of the umbrel. Queen Anne's lace is a biennial. In the first year it appears as a rosette of leaves close to the ground. In its second year it can grow to over 6' tall. This is when the root is big enough to eat and when the large flower appears. This flower is actually a bunch of small flowers crammed together; later it sets tiny fruits and then seeds. I highly recommend going to the World Carrot Museum's website, for here you will find recipes for wild carrot cake, Queen Anne's Lace cognac cocktail (better be of drinking age for this one), plus all the medicinal uses to which it's been put and there are plenty. You will learn more about the wild carrot than you ever thought you wanted to know. Since it is an introduced, very invasive plant (one of the characteristics of weeds), I probably should have included this plant in my book *The A to Z Book of Weeds and Other Useful Plants* rather than here. But it is a beautiful sight in the summertime.

Cool Fact: There are several versions of where the name originated. One is that Queen Anne of England (1655-1714) pricked her finger while making lace, hence the single purple or blood red flower found at the center of the flower head. The poet and naturalist Geoffrey Grigson, however, insisted that the name comes not from Queen Anne but from Saint Anne, the mother of the Virgin Mary, and the patron saint of lace-makers.

What other wildflowers begin with Q?

R

is for

Ratibida
columnifera
Mexican Hat

Michael Emery

R is for *Ratibida columnifera,* Mexican Hat, Longheaded Coneflower, Thimbleflower, Aster Family (Asteraceae)

Ratibida columnifera is the Latin name of yet another member of the huge Sunflower family (Asteraceae). Probably its most common name is Mexican Hat, although you can see where its other names come from. It is also another wildflower that can be seen growing for miles along the Texas roadways beginning in the spring into the summer and even into the first frost if it has water. They will just suddenly appear after a rain as if they have been hiding. The amount of red to yellow can vary quite a lot making it hard to distinguish it from the clasping-leaf coneflower but don't worry too much, they're all in the family. Butterflies enjoy them and a tea from the leaves can be drunk as a beverage or, it's said, to cure a headache. Finches eat the seeds.

Cool Fact: The Zuni Indians use an infusion of the whole plant as an emetic. An infusion is where the parts of the plant are steeped for days, weeks or months in water, oil or alcohol to extract its medicinal properties. The resulting liquid is then used in a variety of ways. So, if you need to vomit for any reason, grab some Mexican hat!

What other wildflowers start with R?

S

is for

SNOW-ON-THE MOUNTAIN

Euphorbia marginata

Michael Emry

S

is for SNOW-0N-THE-MOUNTAIN, *Euphorbia marginata,* Spurge family
Pronunciation yoo- FOR-bee-ah mar-jin-AH-tah
See also, Snow-on-the-Meadow.

Snow-on-the-mountain comes along in Texas just when everything is dried out and wasted. It will cover acres of overgrazed pasture, rising from 10 inches to nearly 5 feet tall. From the single stem branches of various lengths sprout the lovely white clusters of tiny flowers. What appear to be five white petals are actually appendages that surround the very small flowers. With their white bordered leaves, they could be seen as miniature snow-covered mountain ranges. Since the temperatures can be in the 100°F's when they flower, perhaps that's really just wishful thinking. Snow-on-the-mountain is another of those flowers you might not think of looking at but close up they are very pretty. Enjoy this touch of color but be careful, the abundant milk-like sap that oozes from a broken stem irritates the skin and causes dermatitis in some people. On the plus side, spurges have many medicinal uses. That sap or latex will remove warts if you dab a little on but be careful! It's a pretty drastic remedy and can take skin off where you might not have wanted. Snow-on-the-meadow is similar, only the leaves are narrower and the plant is smaller all round.

Cool Fact: The poinsettia, with the red and green leaves, also in the Euphorbia family, is named for Joel R. Poinsett, who while serving as a United States diplomat in Mexico took cuttings of the plant to bring back to his home in South Carolina. In Mexico the poinsettia was called the "Christmas Eve Flower" and it soon became a fixture in the United States. What would Christmas be without the poinsettia?

What other wildflowers start with S?

T is for TRUMPET VINE

Campsis radicans

Michael Evans

T is for TRUMPET VINE, Trumpet Creeper, *Campsis radicans*, (Bignoniaceae)

Trumpet vine or trumpet creeper is a woody vine that despite its attractive orange red flowers, and its ability to bloom all summer long, is not liked by a lot of people; although hummingbirds love it. It doesn't twine in the way that honeysuckle or morning glory do but climbs by means of multiple aerial rootlets that grow into the tree it has decided to climb, (radicans means, "with stems that take root"). It can creep along the ground till it finds a host then climb to 30 feet or more. It gets to be a pest if you don't want it taking over your tree. If it is not regularly pruned it can dismember the tree, telephone pole or whatever else it becomes attached to. The up to three-and-a-half inch long flowers give way to six-inch long pods. They split apart to release the seeds which are flattened and have membranous wings, enabling them to fly on the wind to new grounds. All parts of the plant are toxic and can cause severe skin rash if touched. Trumpet creeper is native to the eastern United States. Like a lot of things, it wasn't born in Texas but it got here as soon as it could. In 1694 it was mistakenly placed in the genus Bignonia, being named for Jean-Paul Bignon. Although extricated from that genus by Alice M. Coats in 1964, you will still see it listed as Bignoniaceae.

Cool Fact: The form *C. radicans* f. *flava* gained the Royal Horticultural Society's Award of Garden Merit. John Wedgwood of the Wedgwood Pottery family first suggested there be a horticultural society in 1800. It wasn't until 1804 that he and his friends had a meeting and founded the Horticultural Society of London. It was granted a royal charter in 1861 and became the Royal Horticultural Society. The Chelsea Flower Show, the most famous of the Society's annual flower shows, attracts people from all over the world.

What other wildflowers start with T?

U is for *Utricularia inflata*

Floating Bladderwort

U is for *Utricularia inflata* and *radiata,* Floating Bladderwort, Bladderwort Family (Lentibulariaceae)

Utricularia inflata is the larger of the two, *radiata* the smaller. *Inflata* refers to the inflated bladders, and *radiata* because of the radial arms that support the plant in the water. But floating bladderwort will best describe the plant, unless perhaps you are talking to a Latin scholar. This interesting plant floats in standing water or shallow, slow moving streams. You might also find it in freshwater marshes or in roadside ditches. Up to ten hollow ribs radiate out from the stem at water level. These spokes or branches are covered with root-like filaments that themselves are covered in microscopic bladders, (*utriculus* means "small bladder"). The leafless stem rises up to 6 inches above the water and bears from 3 to 14 flowers. All the bladderworts in this family live in or near water. The seeds of some bladderworts can be used as a peppery seasoning. They are sometimes called "popweed" because the bladder pods pop when stepped on.

Cool Fact: Those tiny bladders each have complex, delicate valve systems that open when small water animals (the kind you would rather not know are in the water) brush against the sensitive filaments. In a fraction of a second the walls of the bladder spring outward and suck in the protozoa, water flea or minute crustacean passing by. I'm sorry children but, that's right, the Floating Bladderwort is carnivorous! Feed me Seymour!! Although humans have caused some carnivorous plants to become extinct there remain some 670 species and subspecies worldwide.

What other wildflowers start with U?

V is for **VERBENA**

Verbenaceae

Vervain

Michael Emery

V is for VERBENA, (Verbenaceae), Texas Verbena, Prairie Verbena, Dakota Vervain
Pronunciation; ver-BEE-nah

Verbena, Vervain, which is it? Take your pick. Trailing ones tend to be called verbenas and erect ones vervain. Confused yet? *V. bipinnatifida,* now *G. bipinnatifida,* is the most abundant in Texas as far as distribution and period of flowering. Although both are now classified in the genus *Gladularia* the common name verbena is still used. Sprawling or erect they are equally attractive. That purplish-blue, reddish-purple or is it violet blue, is hard to capture when you're painting. The changing light of day tells you one thing one moment then another later. There are pale blue and lavender verbenas too.

Though you won't find it happening today, verbena was used for hundreds of years to cure and treat any number of ailments. The Egyptians, Greeks, and Romans used it in divination, among other things, while in many European countries it was used as a love potion and to ward off evil. When the first settlers came to America they found the Native Americans were using it for many ailments too. Would it confuse you further to know that Frog-fruit, Texas Lantana and American Beautyberry are also in the family? This family includes 3000 species of herbs, shrubs and trees. Teak being one of them.

Cool Fact: The large fruited Sand-verbena, found only in Freestone, Leon and Robertson counties in east-central Texas, is on both the Federal and Texas endangered species list. It is not a verbena, however, it's in the Four-o'clock family. Why Four-o'clock? It only begins to open in the late afternoon and blooms during the night.

What other wildflowers start with V?

W is for

WINE-CUP
Callirhoe
involucrata

Michael Emry

W is for WINE-CUP, *Callirhoe involucrata,* Mallow family (Malvaceae)
Pronunciation: kal-uh-ROH-ee in-voh-loo-KRAY-tah

Wine-cup, both *C. involucrata* and *C. digitata,* the red wine-cups, are the more familiar members of the mallow family, partly because they have been added to the wildflowers sown along the Texas highways. There are 10 or 12 wine-cup or poppy-mallow species within the malvaceae family which includes hibiscus, wild hollyhock, Turk's cap and a thousand more. (If you're not a red wine type there is also a white wine-cup.) The mallow family has provided food and medicine worldwide throughout history. In fact, the spongy pulp of the roots of the marshmallow, boiled down with sugar, made a candy for treating sore throat or bronchitis. The marshmallows found in the store descended from that medicine, although mallow roots no longer form any part of the ingredients. If you wanted to try making your own marshmallows, all of the malvaceae family contain the same properties as the marshmallow. You'll find a recipe in Euell Gibbons' book, *Stalking the Healthful Herbs*. Just don't pick the wine-cups along the highway; you might get a ticket. The next time you are passing a field of cotton or okra, stop and take a look at the flowers. You'll know right away they are in the mallow family too. Hibiscus, another member, combined with lemon grass, is my favorite tea. It is high in vitamin C and in some countries, it is used for a number of health problems. The dried buds of the hibiscus flower are gathered for making tea but this highly popular flower has been cultivated until there are now double blooms and blooms as big as a baby's head.

Cool Fact: *Callirhoe* is a misspelling of Callirrhoe. Callirrhoe is one of the outermost moons of the planet Jupiter. Like the wine-cup it is named for Callirrhoe, the daughter of the river god, Achelus. She was one of Zeus's (Jupiter to the Romans) many conquests. He certainly sowed his wild oats. Don't bother looking for Callirrhoe, the planet Jupiter is 2.5 billion times brighter than its little moon.

What other wildflowers start with W?

X
is for

Xanthisma
texanum
Sleepy Daisy

X is for *Xanthisma texanum* var. *drummondii,* Sleepy Daisy, Star of Texas, Aster Family (Asteraceae)
Pronunciation; zan-THEEZ-mah tex-AN-um

Xanthisma. Boy! It's not easy to find a plant name that begins with X, or anything else, for that matter! Luckily, the practice of using Latin names in botany helps out a bit. *Xanthisma texanum,* let's just say the sleepy daisy, likes to grow anywhere there is sand—from the Panhandle to the Gulf Coast and from the Eastern Cross Timbers to the Rio Grande Valley. From a single stem each plant branches several times, carrying a number of lemon-yellow flowers on each branch. It usually grows to about one to one-and-a-half feet but can reach three feet high. You don't have to be a genius to figure out why it's called sleepy daisy. It doesn't open up till after lunch then closes again in the late afternoon, kind of like its cousin, Lazy Daisy; same thing, only it's white. They look great together if you can catch them while they're open.

Cool Fact: You may have noticed "var. *drummondii*" a few times. Those varieties are named for Thomas Drummond (1790 - 1835). He was a Scotsman who spent nearly two years collecting plants in Texas. Can you imagine how difficult that was back then? The plants he collected were the first from Texas to be distributed to scientific institutions and museums around the world.

What other wildflowers start with X?

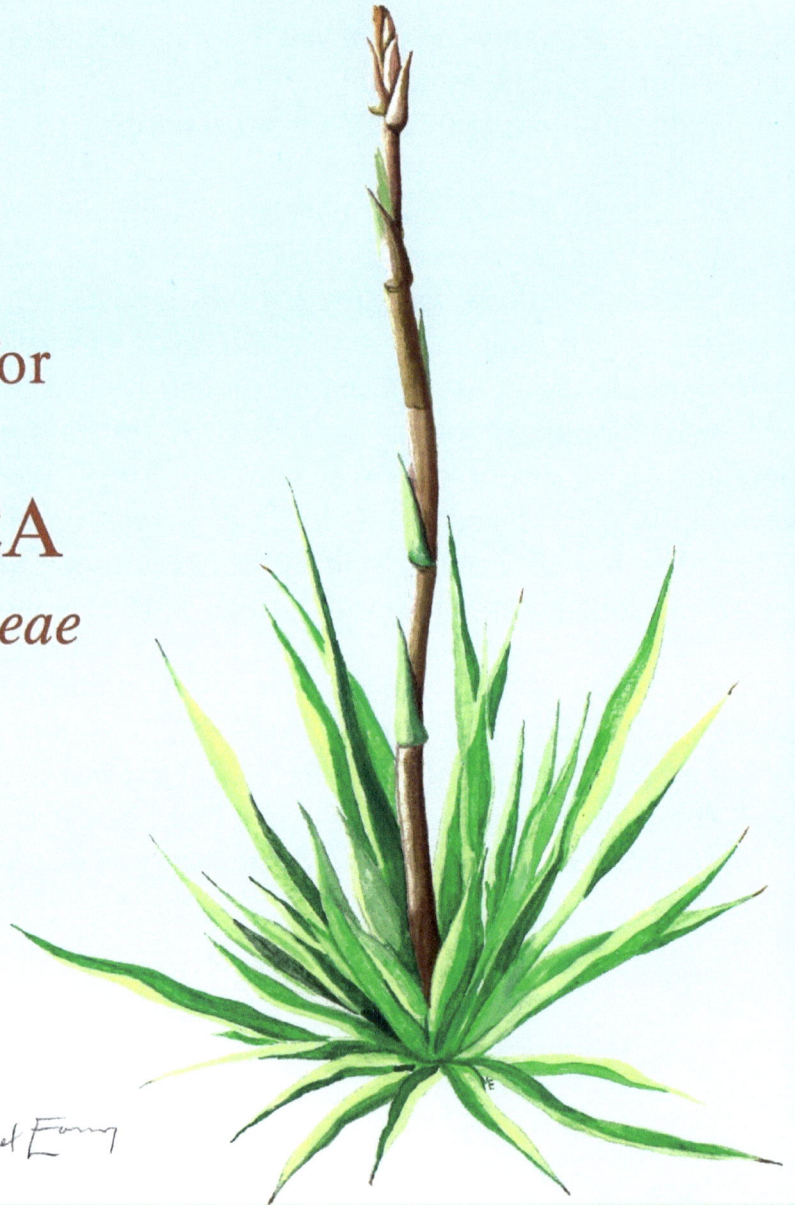

Y

is for

YUCCA

Asparagaceae

Michael Emery

Y is for YUCCA, *Yucca* species, (Asparagaceae) Spanish Dagger, Spanish Bayonet, Soapweed

Yuccas come in many different sizes. There are around twenty native species in Texas, and they all have those sharp pointed leaves you don't want to run into. That explains the first two common names. Soapweed comes from the fact that yucca root can be used for washing. The root is dug up, cleaned, mashed with a hammer or a rock, placed in the wash bucket and stirred. In New Mexico I've seen it used for the annual washing of the natural wool used in a home-made comforter. Once the wool is dry it's laid out on a sheet and beaten with a dried yucca stalk to fluff it up, after which it's stuffed back into the comforter, ready for the coming winter. It can also be used as a shampoo or for washing yourself. The yucca has been used for thousands of years throughout the Southwest and Mexico: the fiber being used for making rope, baskets, sandals and any number of other things. The deer will eat the sprouting stalk of the yucca unless it's almost inaccessible—like on the side of a cliff. It's like a large asparagus but you really shouldn't eat them at that stage as the flowers are edible and high in vitamin C, as are the fruits that follow. The pods are often roasted or made into a conserve and even fermented to make an alcoholic drink. In all ways the Yucca has proved to be a friend to man, as long as he doesn't walk into it.

Cool Fact: The Yucca is a perfect example of the ways in which nature has provided for the continuation of a species; a balance that mankind constantly puts in jeopardy. A small white moth is the only creature responsible for the pollination of the Yucca; a different species of moth for each species of yucca. In a very complex procedure, the Yucca moth lays its eggs on the pistil of the plant. These eggs develop along with the plant's seeds, upon which the larvae feed. The larvae eat only enough to develop to their next stage, leaving sufficient seeds to grow into new plants. No moth, no more yucca. Illustration is of the Twist-leaf Yucca or Texas yucca, *Yucca rupicola*.

What other wildflowers start with Y?

Z
is for

Zeltnera
beyrichii
Mountain Pink

Michael E——

Z is for *Zeltnera beyrichii,* Gentian family, (Gentianaceae), Mountain Pink

Mountain Pink seldom grow more than 10 inches high, forming such a lovely bouquet of flowers you could just snip the stem and do no more, except maybe add a bow. It often grows in rocky limestone which can be a challenge. A plant two inches high with only one or two flowers is not uncommon. I prefer to leave it be, as it is a big treat to find it at all in Texas. A good rain in the spring will bring many to flower, and they will continue to flower well after the dry weather sets in, but in a dry year you may have trouble finding any. The genus *Zeltnera* has 25 species that are native to the Americas and are not found anywhere else in the world. Until 2004 the mountain pink was known as *Centaurium beyrichii*. Then a closer look at its DNA caused the name change. One common name for this plant is Catchfly because the stem exudes a sticky sap that traps any small insect come to cause mischief, such as eating its stems or leaves.

Cool Fact: "Moxie" means to be plucky, able to face difficulty with spirit. It comes from the name of a bitter soft drink made with gentian root. "Beverage Moxie Nerve Food" claimed to be a cure for "loss of manhood, helplessness, imbecility and insanity." It outsold Coca-Cola for years. They should start making it again, don't you think?

What other wildflowers start with Z?

Twenty-six flowers are, I hope, sufficient to whet your appetite for discovering more Texas wildflowers, being that there are more than 5,000 flowering plants, at least a thousand of which fall into the category of "wildflowers." I offer one more. Like so many others, it comes from far away but has managed to find a home in Texas.

BOUGAINVILLEA
Paper Flower

BOUGAINVILLEA, *Bougainvillea spectablis,* Paper Flower
Four-o'clock family (Nyctaginaceae)

Bougainvillea is a native of South America but has been spread around the world by its admirers. It comes in yellow, red, orange, mauve, and purple-red. In addition to the many cultivars, hybrids have happened spontaneously. There are now 300 varieties. It's a vine and may grow as high as 40 feet. In San Miguel de Allende, Gto., Mexico, there was a restaurant, appropriately named, La Buganvilia, where one plant had taken over the glass domed interior courtyard dining area. Always accommodating, bougainvillea is evergreen where there is year-round rain, or deciduous where dry seasons occur. It is often made into a bonsai. In Thailand you will see three plants with different colored flowers that have been twined around each other to form one plant. It is easily grown from cuttings and needs to be clipped back often. And watch out for those sharp thorns! When clippings are thrown out it's not surprising they take to the wild where conditions are suitable. Bougainvillea is reported to have anti-inflammatory, anti-bacterial, anti-virus, anti-tumor, anti-hypercholestrolemic, anti-hyperlipidemic, and anti-fertility properties. Whew!

Cool Fact: The botanist Philibert Commerçon named it for French Admiral Louis Antoine Bougainville, having discovered it while accompanying the Admiral during his voyage around the world. It's possible that Jeanne Barré was actually the first European to observe the plant and pointed it out to her companion. Besides being an expert in botany, she was Commerçon's assistant and lover. She made the voyage with Commerçon disguised as a man since women were not allowed on the ship. This way she became the first woman to circumnavigate the earth.

More A to Z Wildflowers;

A. Aster, Acacia, Arrowhead
B. Bleeding Heart, Broomweed, Buttonbush
C. Cardinal Flower, Columbine, Cranesbill
D. Dandelion, Desert Marigold, Day Flower
E. Elderberry, Evolvulus
F. Frogfruit, Flame Orchid
G. Gay Feather, Goldenrod, Gumweed
H. Henbit, Horsemint, Hemlock
I. Iris, Ironweed
J. Jasmine, Johnny-jump-up
K. *Krameria lanceolate*
L. Larkspur, Leather-flower
M. Meadow-pink, Mullein, Mealy Sage
N. Nettle
O. Old-man's-beard, Olive
P. Phlox, Poppy
Q. *Quincula lobate*
R. Rain-lily, Red Buckeye
S. Sumac, Sorrel, Spatterdock
T. Turk's Cap, Thistle
U. Umbrella-wort
V. Violet, Velvet-leaf
W. Water-lily, Wild Onion
X. *Xanthocephalum sarothrae*
Y. Yarrow, Yellow-wisteria
Z. Zinnia

Bibliography:

Geyata, Ajilvsgi. 1984. *Wildflowers of Texas*. Shearer Publishing

Gibbons, Euell. Drawings by Raymond W. Rose. 1966. *Stalking the Healthful Herbs*. David McKay Company

Heying, Heather E. 2002. *Antipode*. St. Martin's Press

Jones, Pamela. Illustrations by Bob Johnson. 1999. *Just Weeds*. Prentis Hall Press

Loflin, Brian & Shirley Loflin. 2009. *Texas Cacti*. Texas A & M Press

Loughmiller, Cambell and Lynn. 1996. *Texas Wildflowers*. University of Texas Press

Poole, Jackie M., William R. Carr, Dana M. Price & Jason R. Singhurst. 2007. *Rare Plants of Texas*. Texas A & M Press

Silverthorne, Elizabeth. 1996. *Legends and Lore of Texas Wildflowers*. Texas A & M Press

Stokes, Donald and Lillian. 1993.*The Wildflower Book*. Little Brown

Tull, Delena. 1987. *Edible and Useful Plants of the Southwest*. University of Texas Press

Wasowski, Sally and Andy Wasowski. 1988. *Native Texas Plants*. Lonestar Books

Wills, Mary Motz. Text by Howard S. Irwin. 1961. *Roadside Flowers of Texas*. University of Texas Press

Zim, Herbert S. and Alexander C. Martin. Illustrations by Rudolf Freund. 1950. *Flowers*. Golden Press, New York

Wikipedia and various other online sites.